A note to parents

This package is designed for children aged 5 upwards. The age  guideline only.

The package provides an introduction to Italian and uses a com children are likely to encounter in everyday situations. The aim i enjoy speaking to an Italian person.

The cassette and book can be used independently, but complement each other in terms of content.
The package is structured so that it focuses on a week in the life of two Italian children, Gina and Marco.

It is interspersed with games and puzzles, rhymes and songs, so as to make the introduction to the new language as fun as possible. Words and phrases are repeated and reinforced throughout.

There is a vocabulary slot at the end of each section to consolidate the words and structures used. The aim is not to labour grammar, but to raise awareness of language patterns.

Your invovlement and interest are of great importance and we hope that the activities will provide many opportunities for conversation between you and your child. Enjoy the package together; the greater the enjoyment, the more your child will gain confidence and the more s/he will benefit. Encourage your child to work in short bursts. Replay each section on the cassette as you think necessary and at a pace to suit your child. Encourage your child to imitate the authentic pronunciation used on the cassette.

 The pencil symbol is used throughout the book to indicate an activity to be completed by the child.

First published 1993 by Pan Macmillan Children's Books
a division of Pan Macmillan Ltd, Cavaye Place, London SW10 9PG

9 8 7 6 5 4 3 2 1

Text © Lucy Duke 1993   Illustrations © Stuart Trotter 1993

ISBN 0 330 32910 3

Printed and bound in Great Britain by Henry Ling Ltd, The Dorset Press, Dorchester
This book is sold subject to the condition that it shall not, by way of trade or otherwise, be lent, re-sold, hired out or otherwise circulated without the publisher's prior consent in any form of binding or cover other than that in which it is published and without a similar condition including this condition being imposed on the subsequent purchaser.
Whilst the advice and information in this book are believed to be true and accurate at the time of going to press, neither the author nor the publisher can accept any responsibility or liability for any errors or omissions that may be made.

Ecco l'Italia!

Fill in the name of the capital of Italy, where Marco lives.

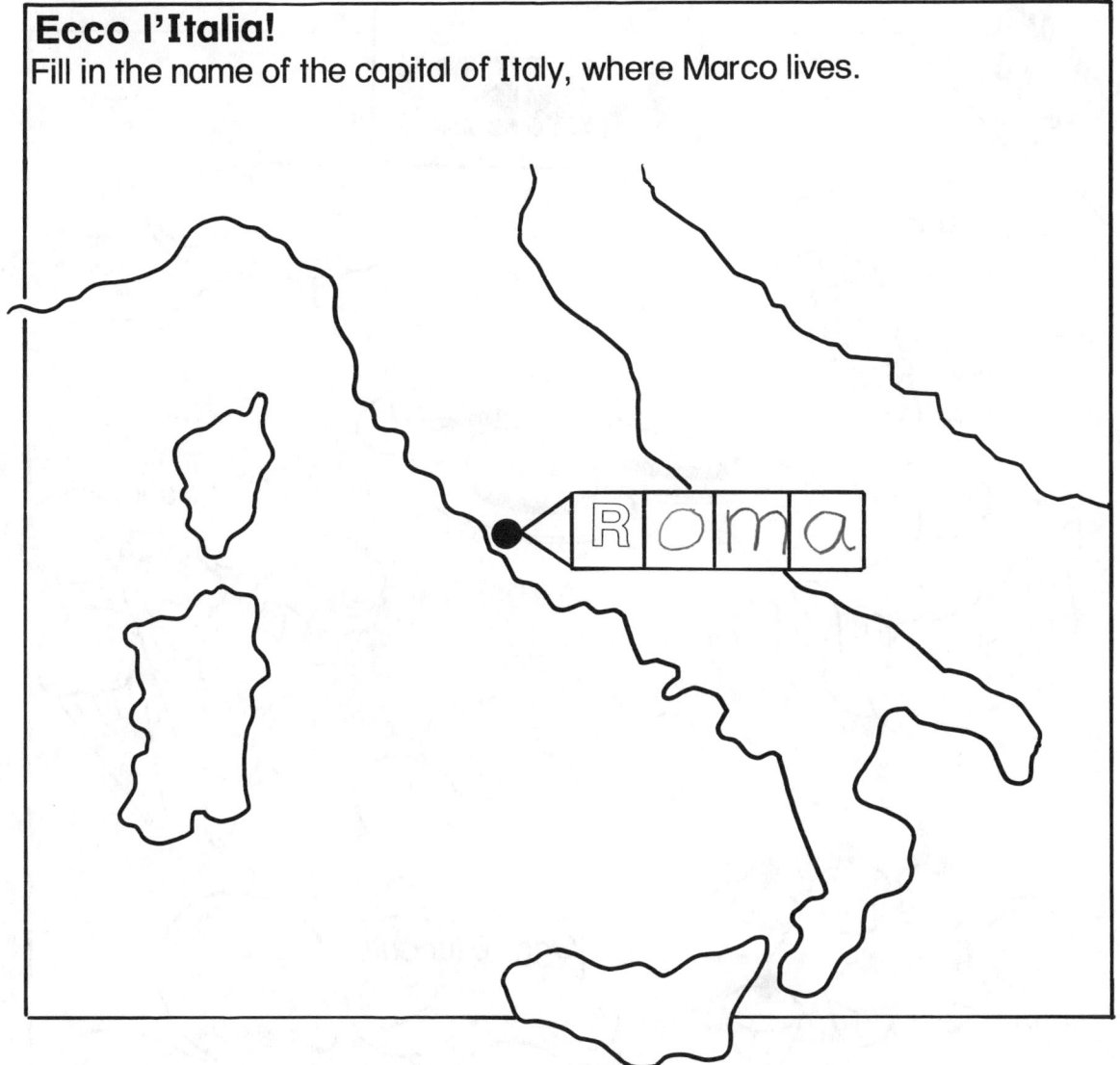

Ciao!	Hello/Hi!
	(You can also say **Ciao** for 'goodbye'!)
Come ti chiami?	What's your name?
Mi chiamo . . .	My name is . . .
Dove abiti?	Where do you live?
Abito a . . .	I live in . . .
Ecco l'Italia!	Here's Italy!
nell'acqua	in the water

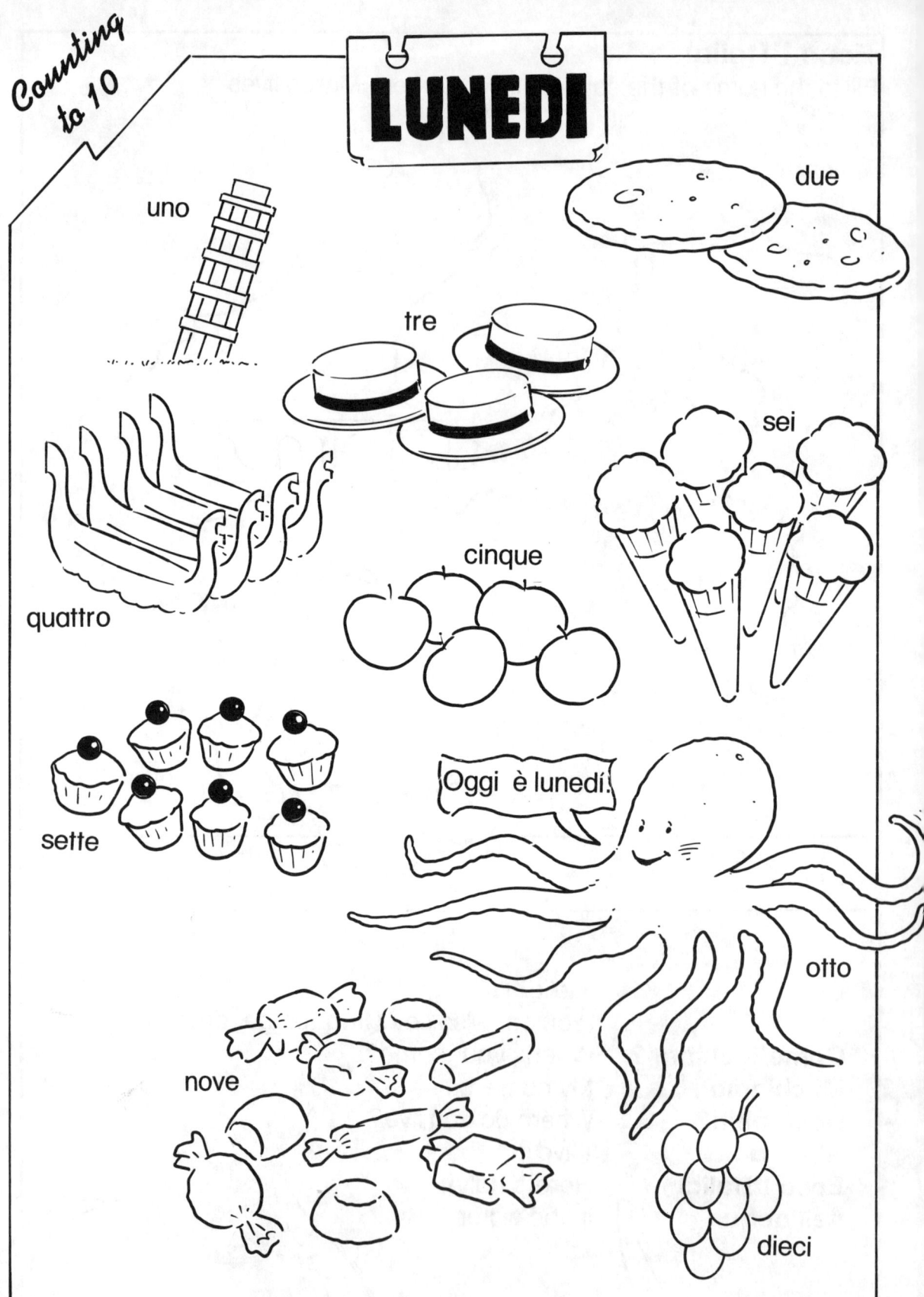

Join the numbers to the words.

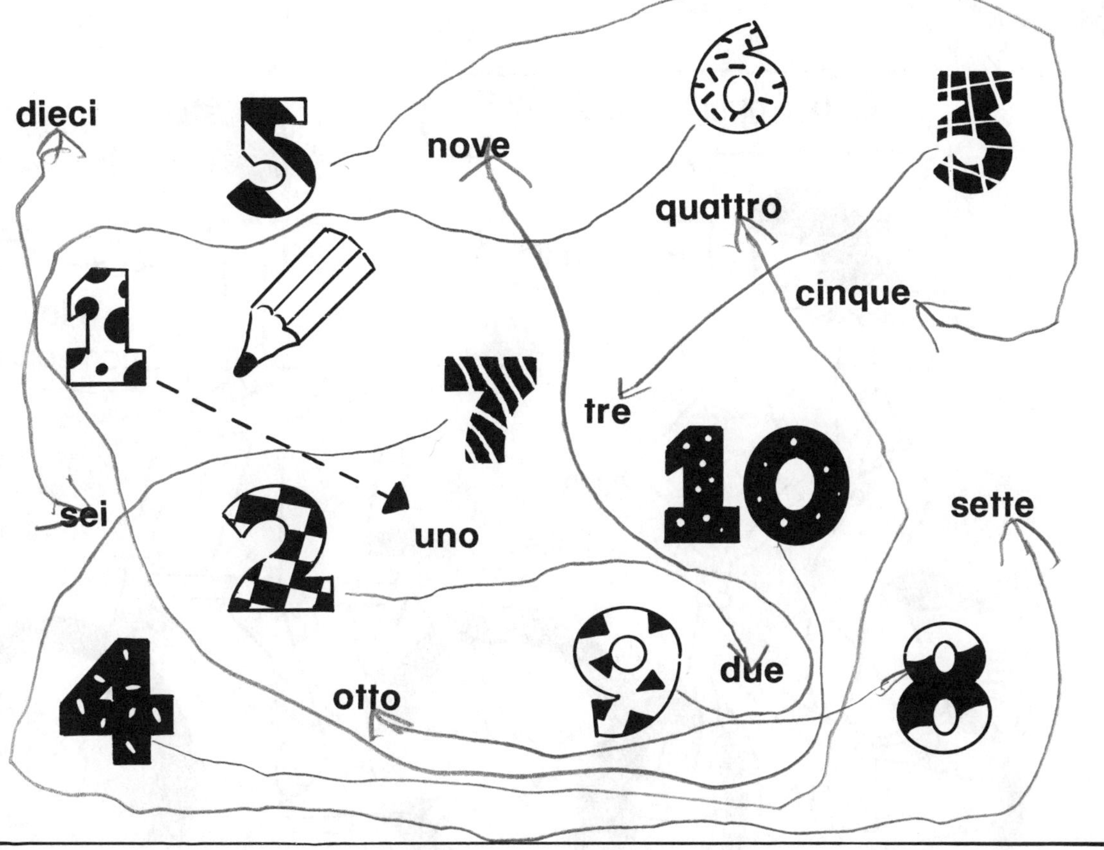

dieci
nove
quattro
cinque
tre
sette
uno
due
otto

Join the dots.
Try counting in Italian as you do it.

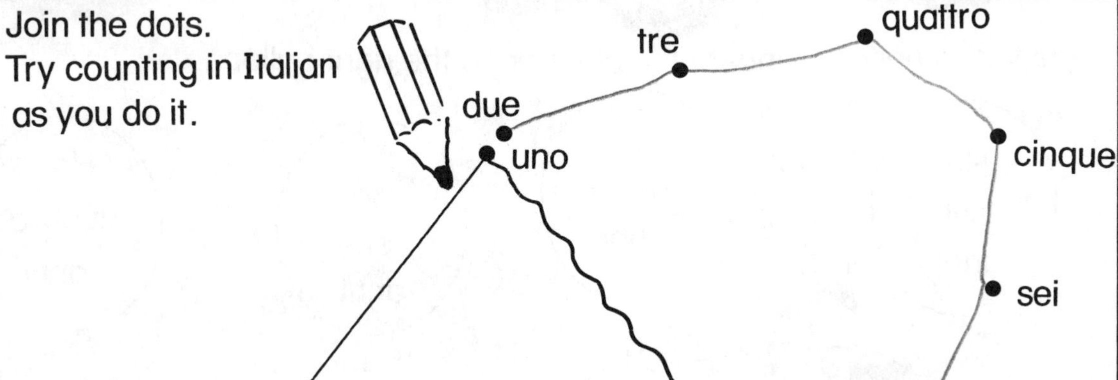

uno
due
tre
quattro
cinque
sei
sette
otto
nove
dieci

Write how old you would be if these were your birthday cakes.

Ho sette anni

Ho tre anni

Ho uno annio

Ho otto ~~uno~~ anni

Oggi è lunedí — Today is Monday
Quanti anni hai? — How old are you?
Ho sei anni — I'm six
Ho dieci anni — I'm ten

Ho quattro anni!

Colour the Italian flag.

verde
bianco
rosso

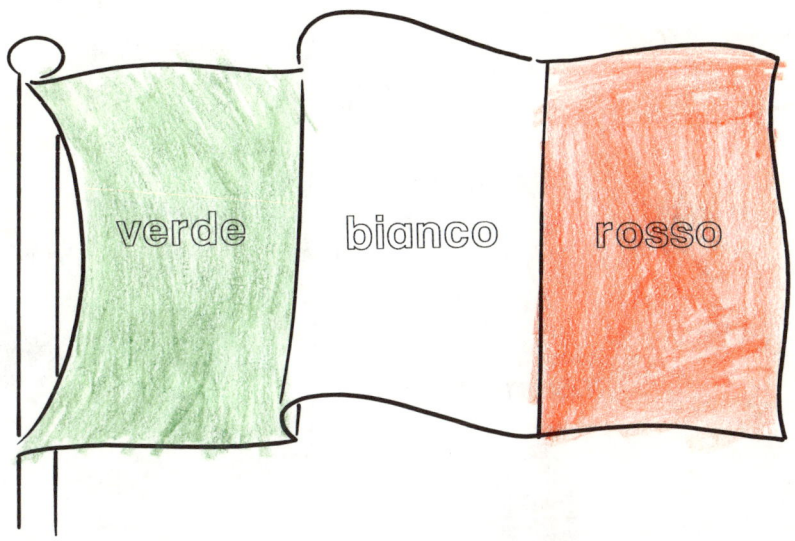

Now colour this picture.

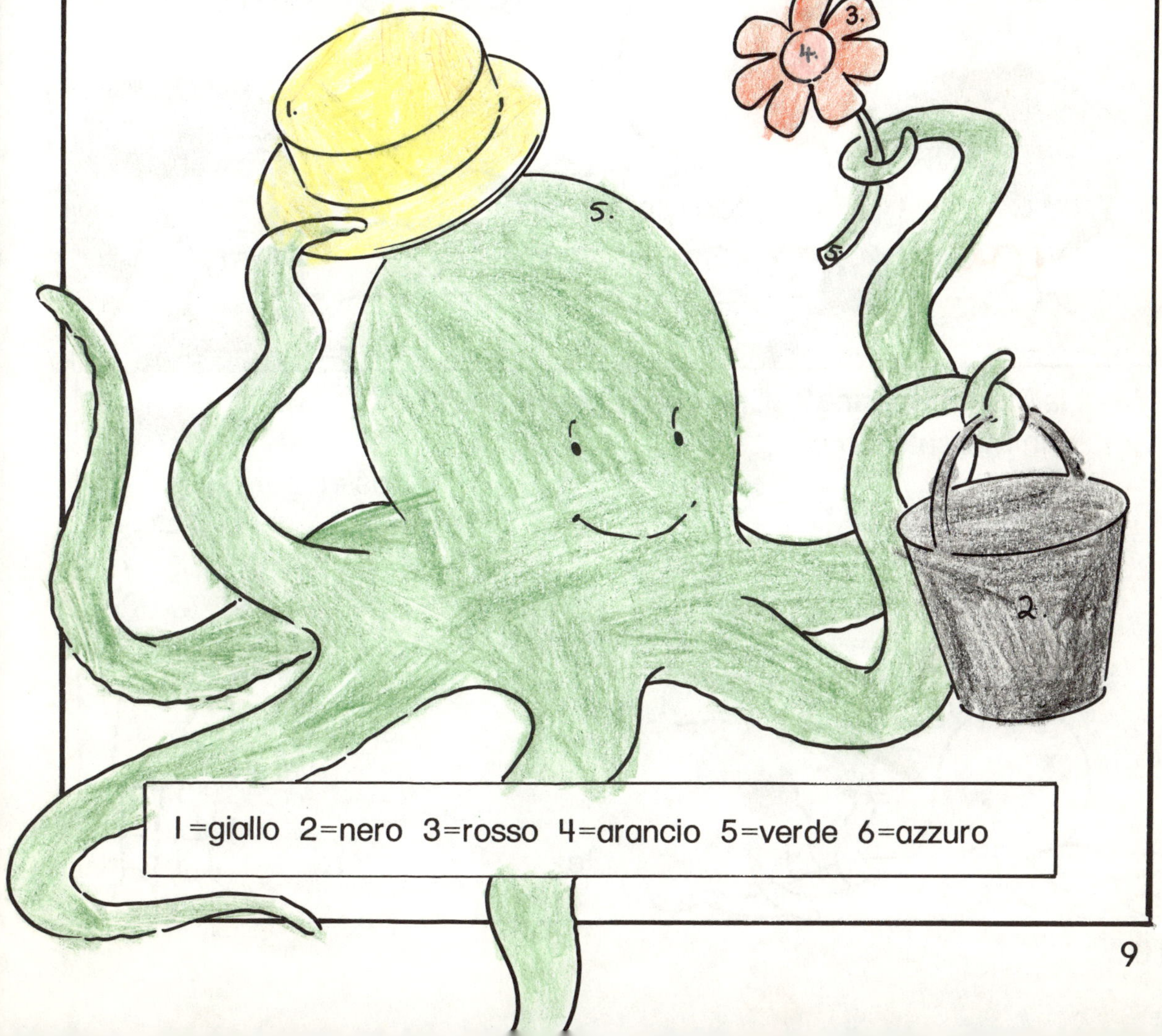
1=giallo 2=nero 3=rosso 4=arancio 5=verde 6=azzuro

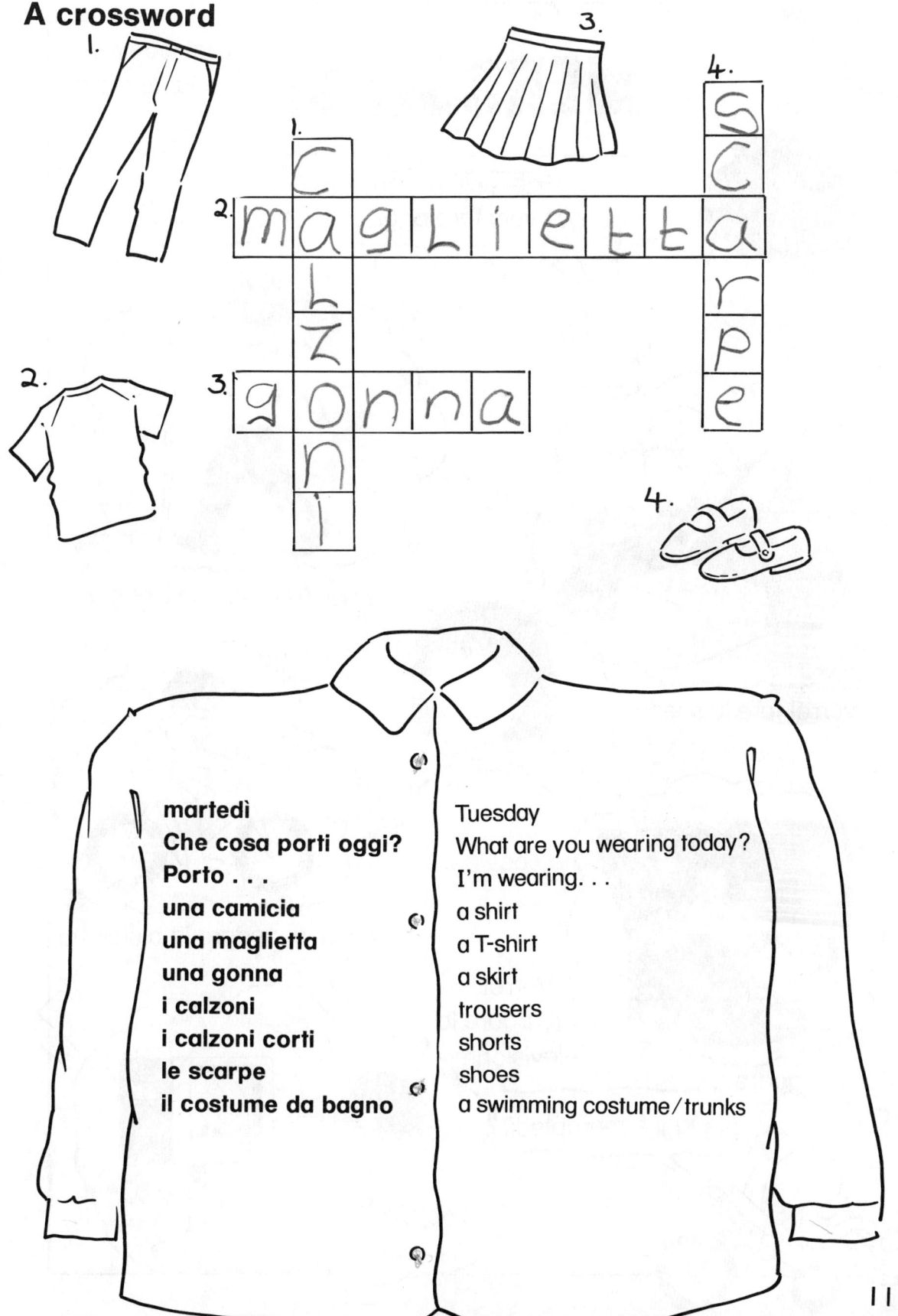

Use the picture clues to help you fill in the missing words.

Fare la _ _ _ _ _

Andare in _ _ _ _ _ _ _ _ _ _ _

Leggere un _ _ _ _ _

Fare una _ _ _ _ _ _ _ _ _ _ _ _

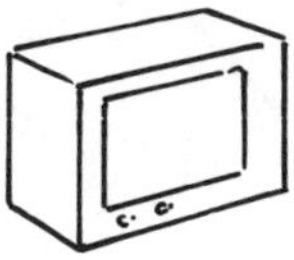

Guardare la _ _ _ _ _ _ _ _ _ _ _

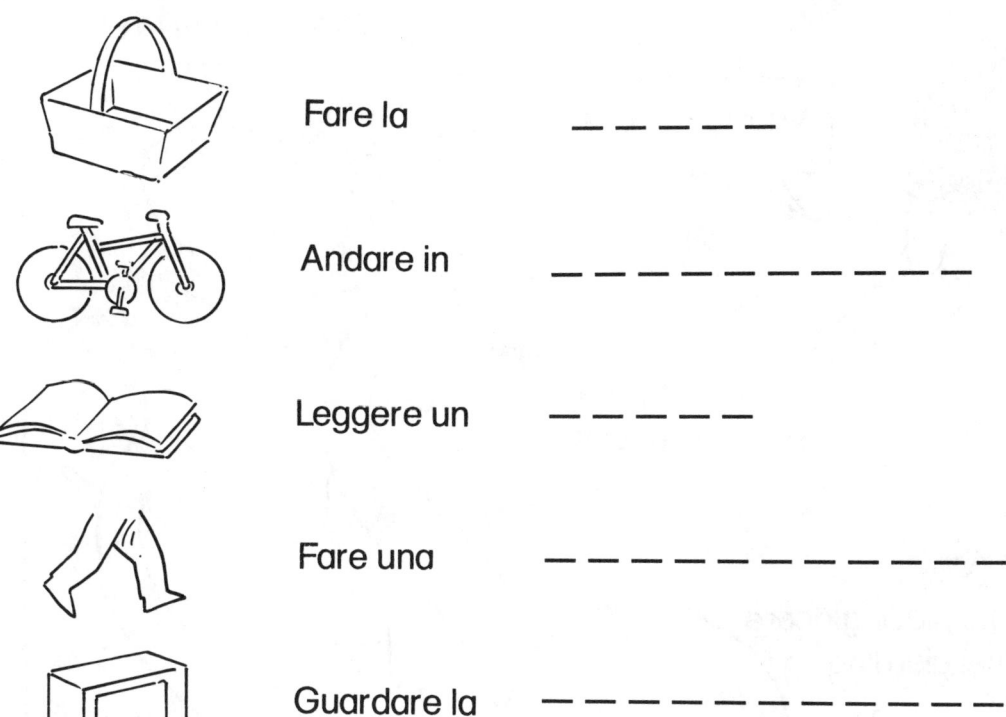

What is Marco going to do today?

Can you say it in Italian?

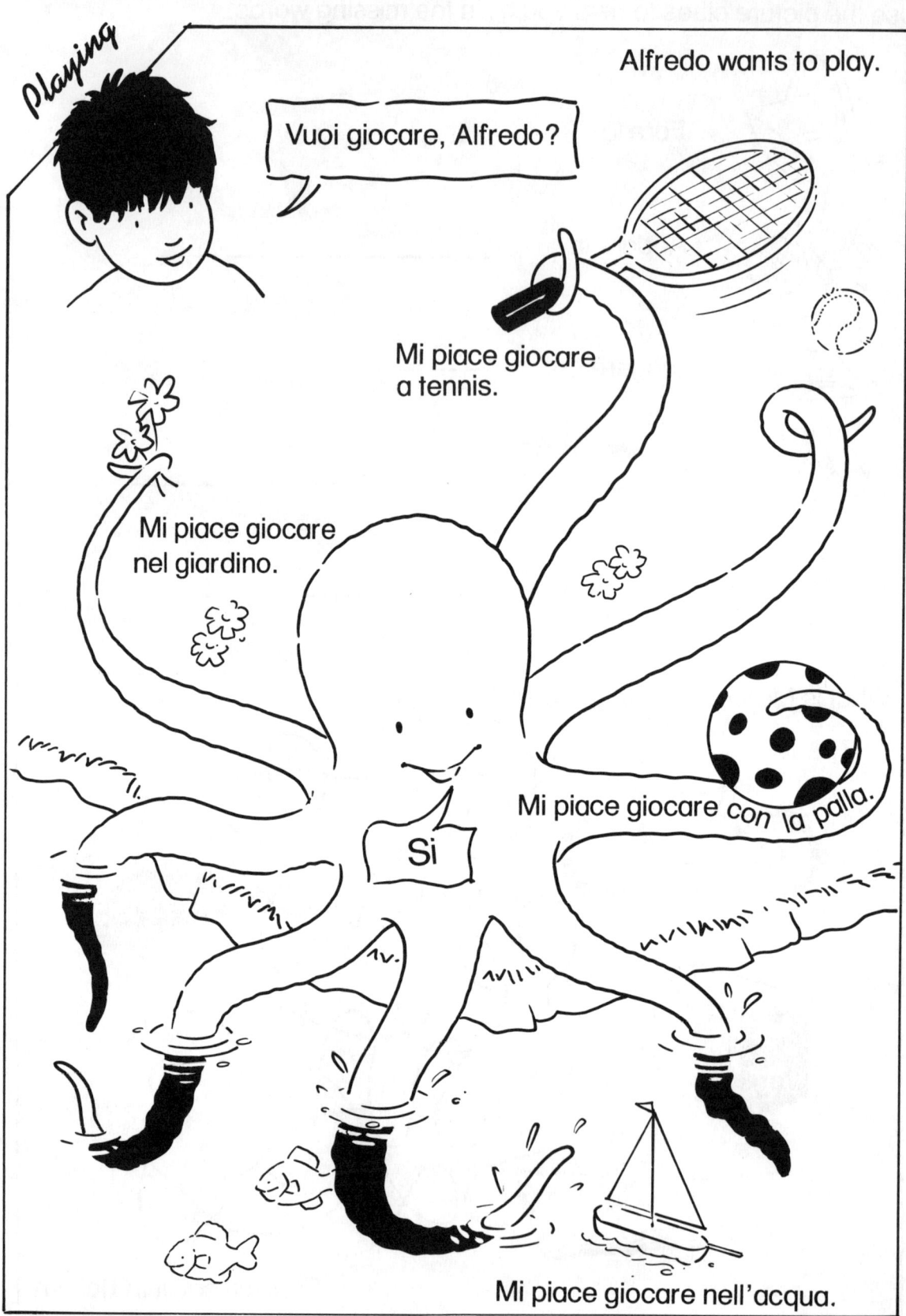

The *Leaning* Tower of Pisa

A game Un gioco

You will need a die and some counters. Every time you land on a square with a picture, try to name it in Italian before you move on.

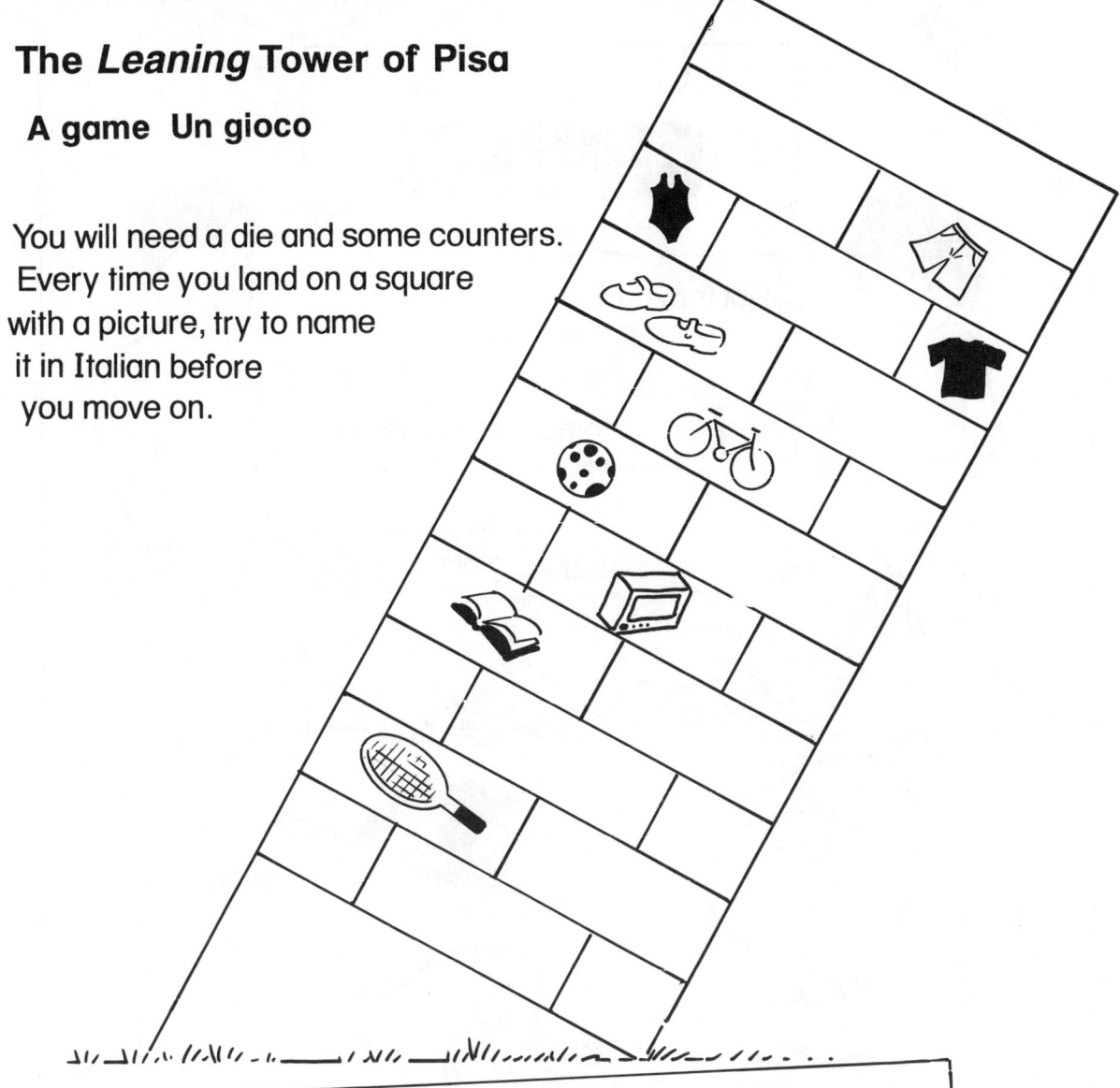

Mercoledí
Che cosa vuoi fare?
Vorrei . . .
Vorrei fare una passeggiata
 . . . fare la spesa
 . . . andare in bicicletta
 . . . leggere un libro .
 . . . guardare la televisione
Mi piace giocare. . .
 . . . con la palla

Wednesday
What would you like to do?
I'd like . . .
I'd like to go for a walk
 . . . to go shopping
 . . . to ride a bike
 . . to read a book
 . . . to watch television
I like playing . . .
 . . . with a ball

15

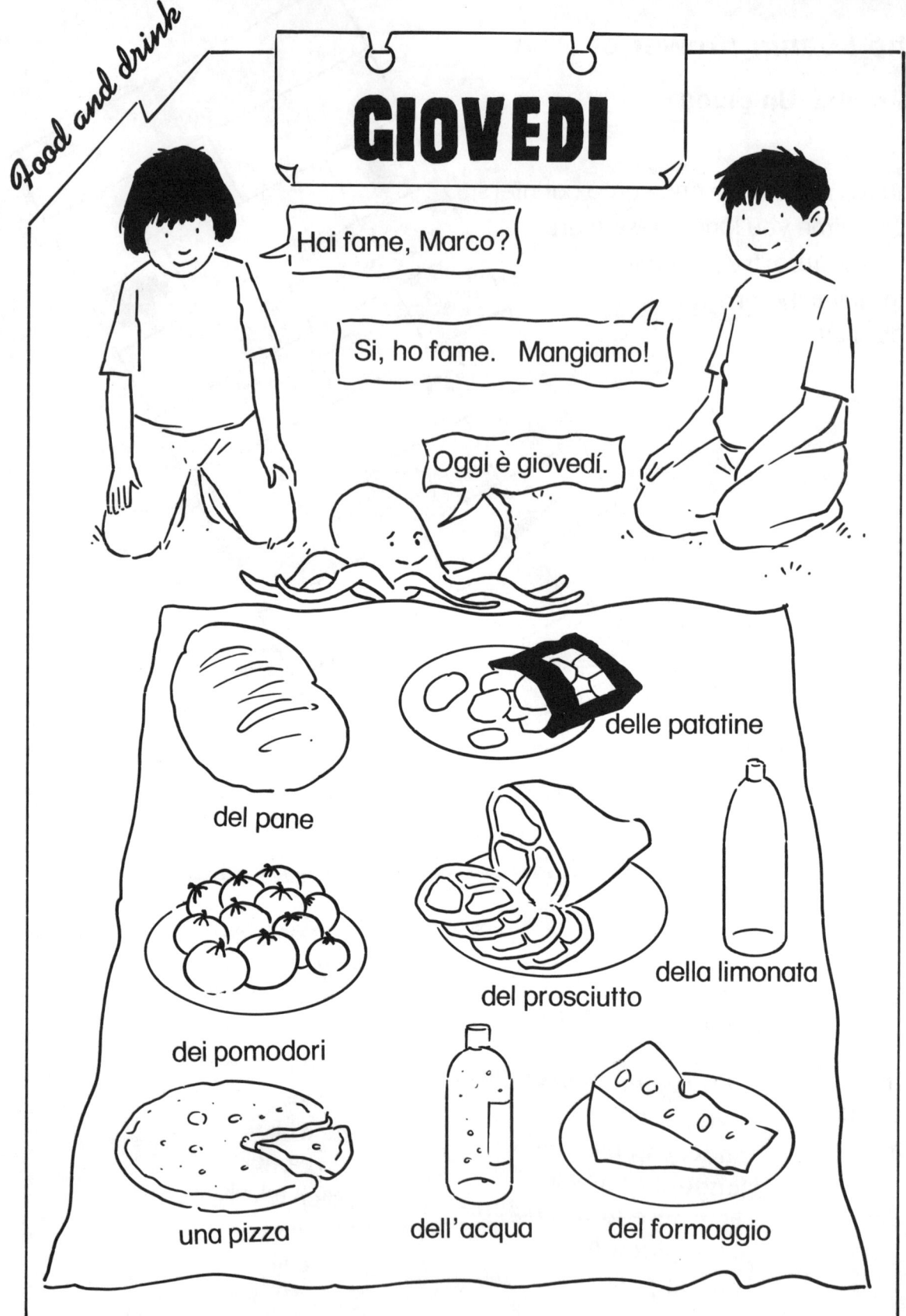

Can you draw the right food on to each plate?

del formaggio

dei pomodori

del pane

Unscramble the letters to fill in the food crossword.

Make your own pizza!

Choose your favourite toppings from the shelf and write them on your pizza. Then draw and colour them. Can you see what the bottom of the pizza is made from?

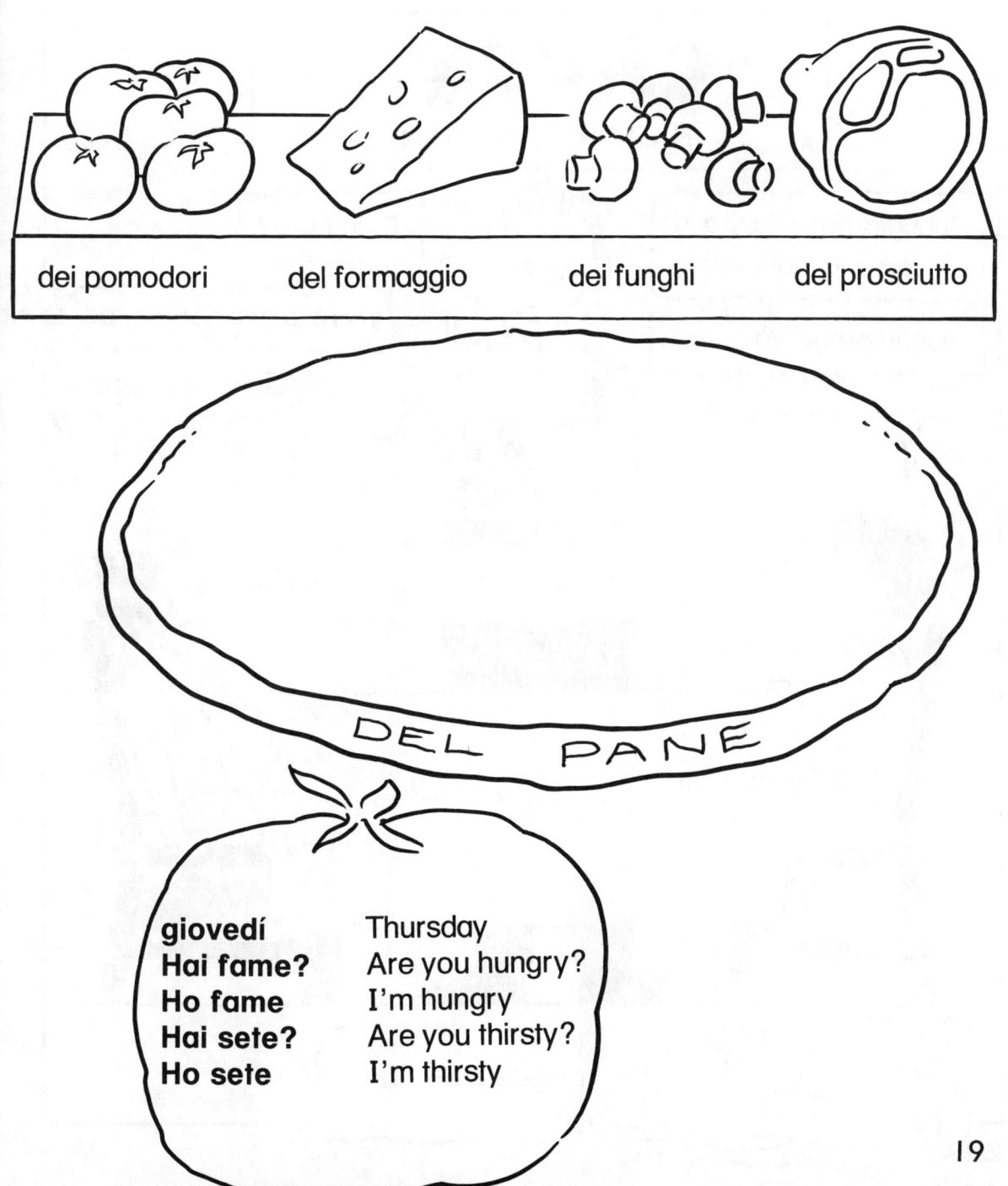

| dei pomodori | del formaggio | dei funghi | del prosciutto |

DEL PANE

giovedí	Thursday
Hai fame?	Are you hungry?
Ho fame	I'm hungry
Hai sete?	Are you thirsty?
Ho sete	I'm thirsty

19

Can you make these match up?

Vorrei una pizza, per favore.
Vorrei del pane, per favore.
Vorrei delle patatine, per favore.
Vorrei una limonata, per favore.

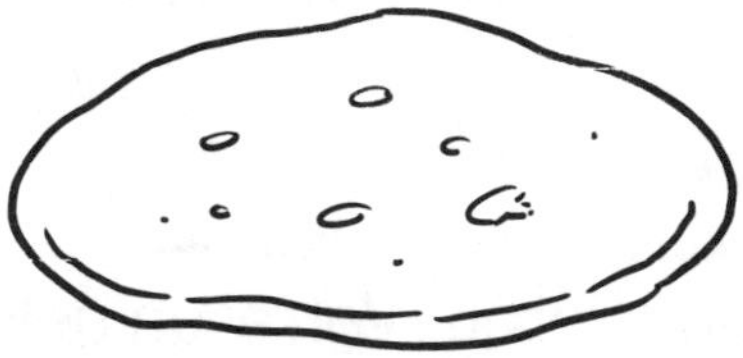

Match the heads and tails of these food words.

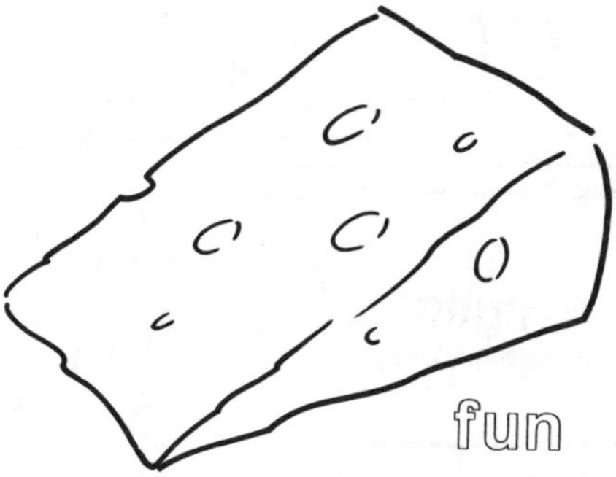

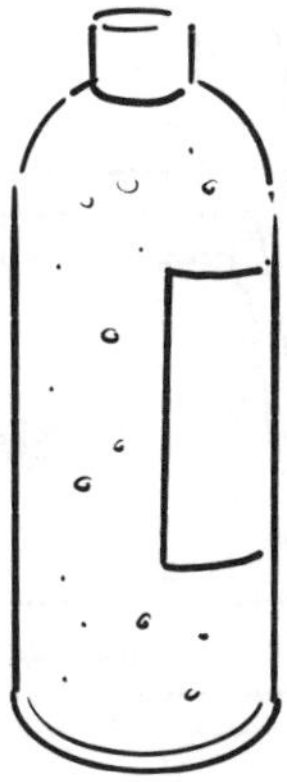

fun   iutto
lim   maggio
prosc   odori
pom   ghi
gel   onata
for   ato

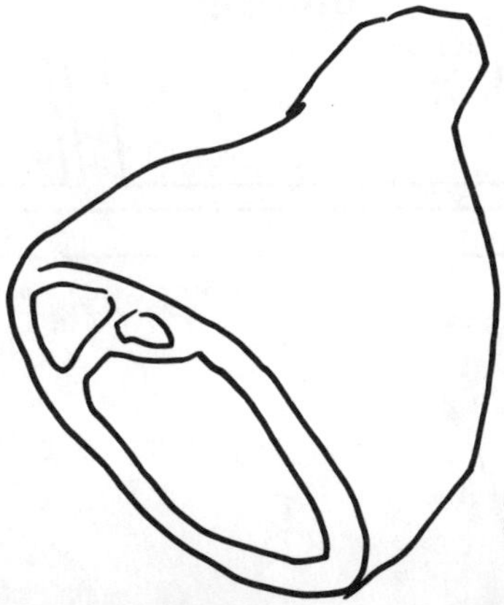

21

What flavour are these ice-creams?

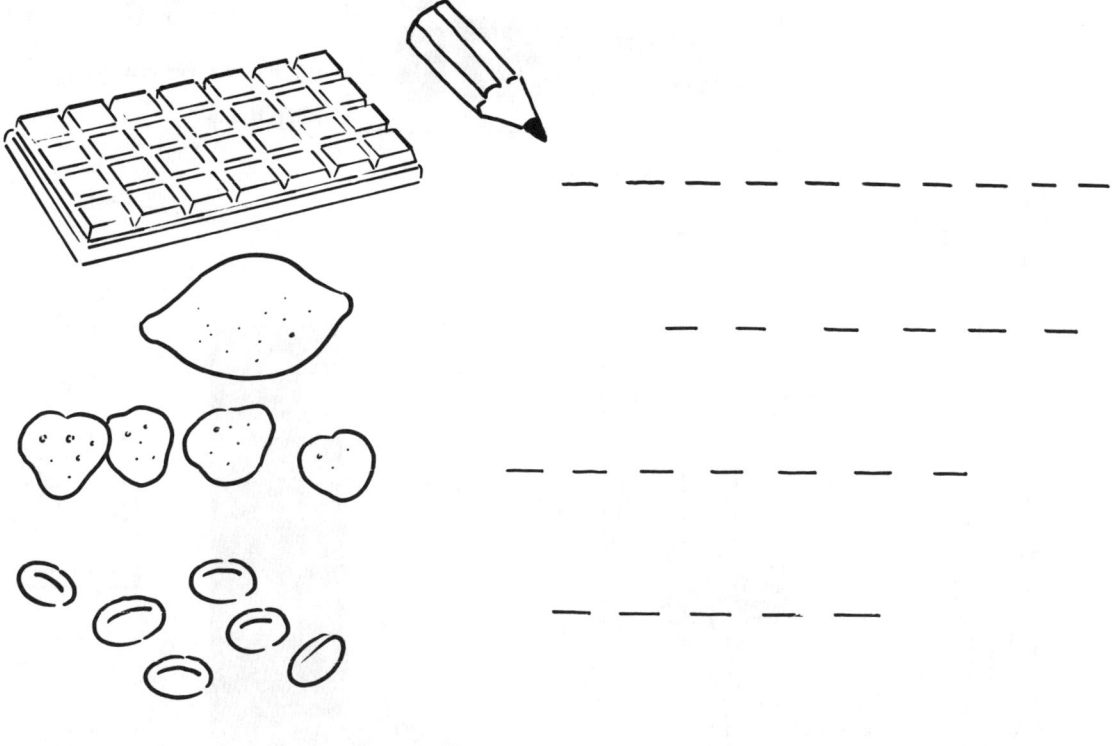

Which is your favourite flavour? _____

venerdí	Friday
Buongiorno, prego?	Hello, can I help you?
per favore	please
grazie	thank you
un gelato al cioccolato	a chocolate ice-cream
fragola	strawberry
limone	lemon
caffè	coffee
vaniglia	vanilla
Buon appetito!	Enjoy your meal!

Follow the lines and fill in the words.

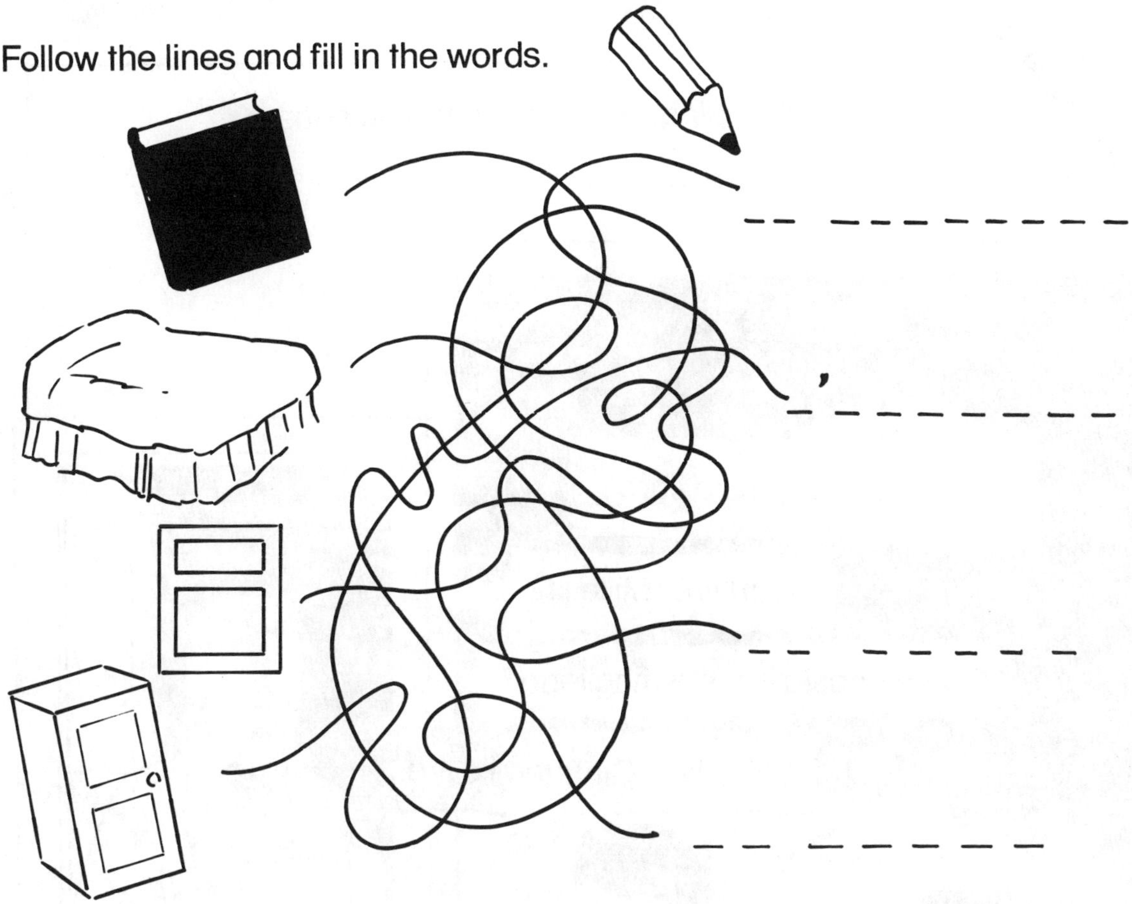

_ _   _ _ _ _ _ _

_ ' _   _ _ _ _ _ _

_ _   _ _ _ _ _

_ _   _ _ _ _ _ _

Can you find the six things from the children's hotel room in this puzzle?

S	G	A	V	V	A	R	O	N	Z	A
Y	H	A	W	D	B	N	L	S	P	R
S	J	R	B	A	R	N	E	Y	S	T
C	A	M	E	R	A	H	T	G	B	S
T	I	A	L	Q	K	U	T	M	A	E
N	W	D	S	U	Z	I	O	Q	G	N
A	C	I	M	R	G	X	S	U	N	I
P	Z	O	X	Y	L	I	B	R	O	F

25

At the shops

Let's go shopping. Andiamo a fare la spesa.

Quanto costa questo libro?

1000 lire. Mille lire.

Quanto costa questa maglietta?

5000 lire. Cinquemila lire.

When you go to Italy, you will need to change your money into Italian lire (say it 'lee-ra') before you can buy anything.

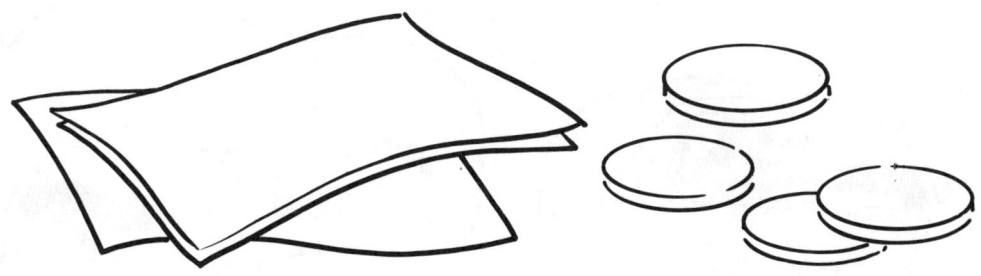

Q _ _ N _ _   C _ S _ _   QUESTO   L _ _ R _ ?

sabato	Saturday
Andiamo . . .	Let's go . . .
la camera	room
il letto	bed
la finestra	window
l'armadio	cupboard/wardrobe
Quanto costa questo...?	How much is this...?

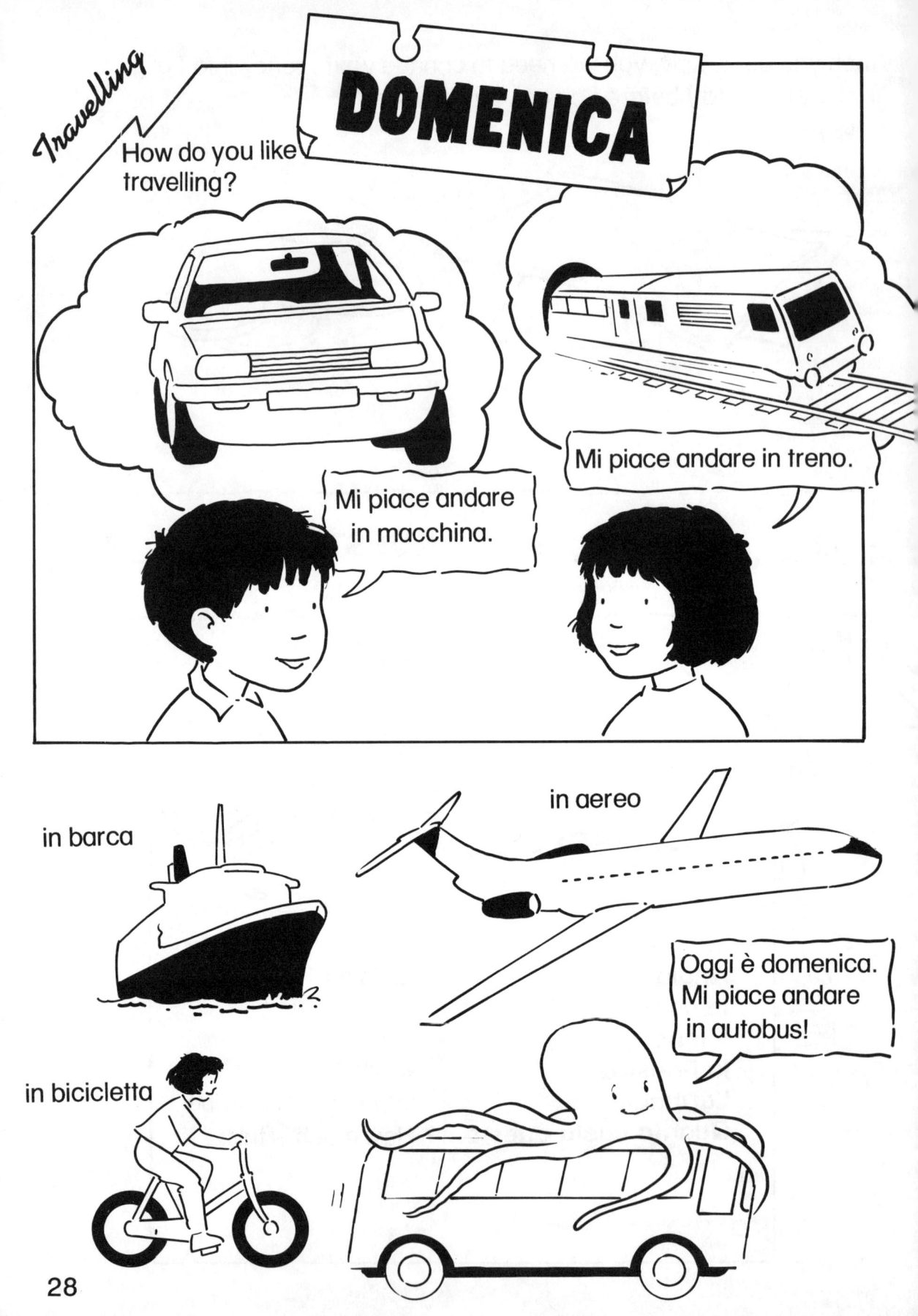

What is Gina saying? Fill in the missing letters.

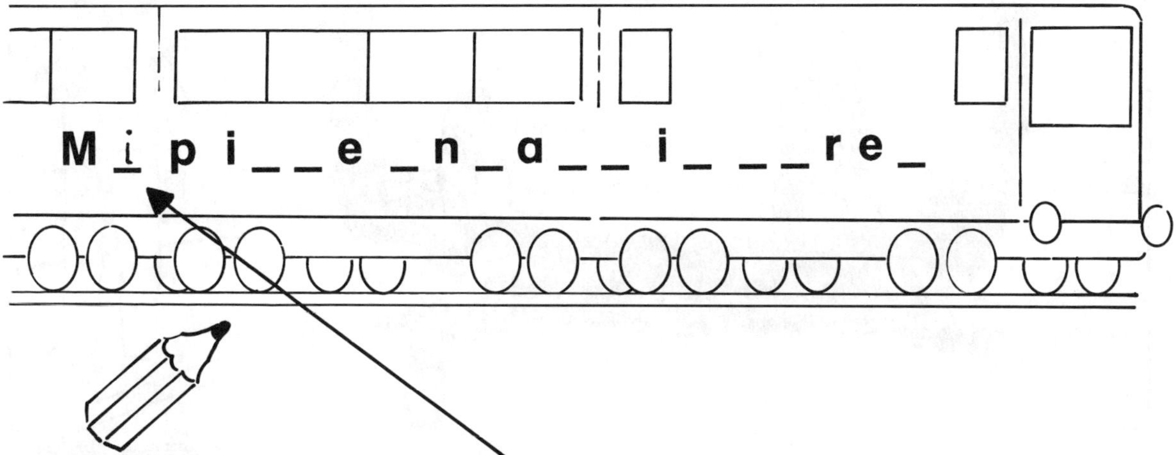

M i p i _ _ e _ n _ a _ _ i _ _ _ r e _

d e e a a i r c a n o

Andiamo!
Find the end of each word

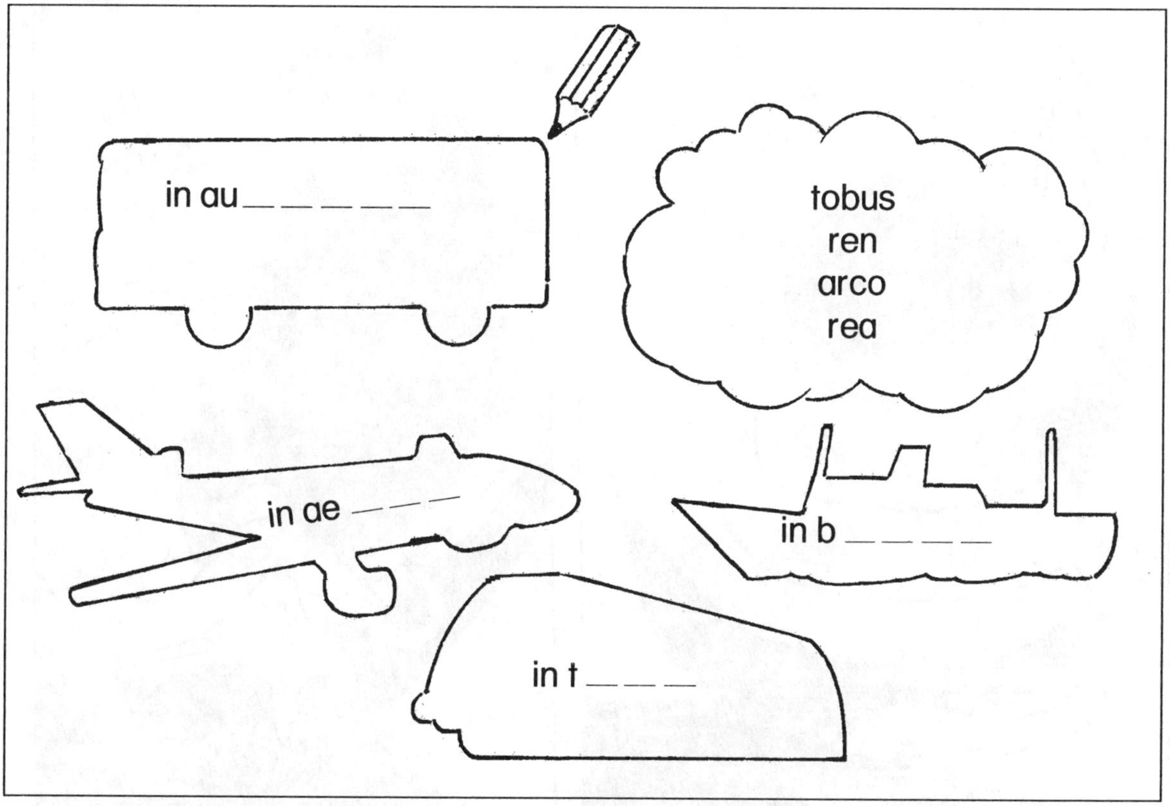

in au _ _ _ _ _ _

tobus
ren
arco
rea

in ae _ _ _ _

in b _ _ _ _ _

in t _ _ _ _

Find your way through the maze and fill in the words. Where is Gina? Dov'è Gina?

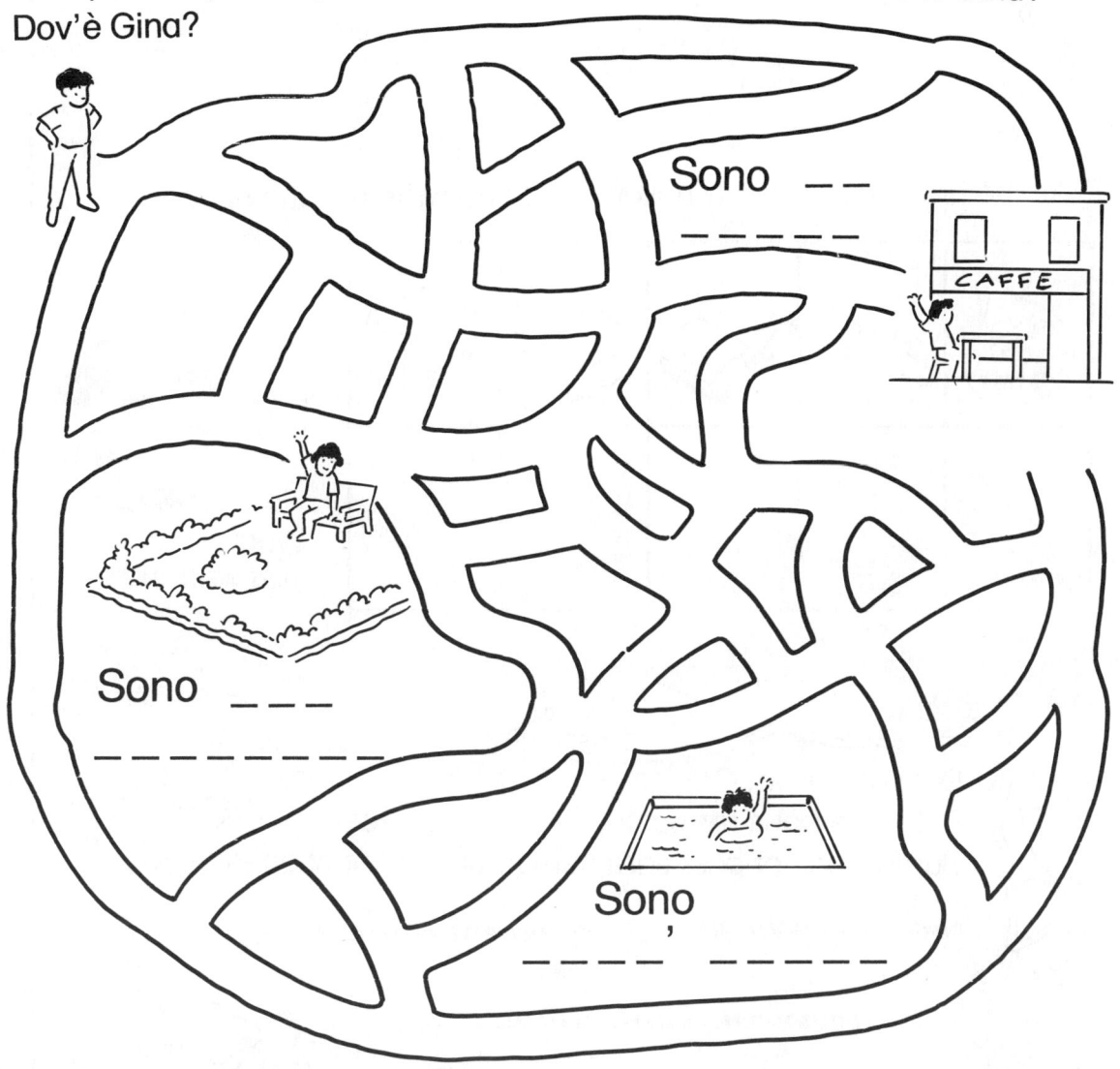

domenica	Sunday
Mi piace...	I like...
Mi piace andare in treno.	I like going by train.
Dov'è Gina?	Where's Gina?
Aiuto!	Help!
nell'acqua	in the water
Sei gentile.	You are kind.

Activity page

Take the first letter of each Italian word and write it in the space.

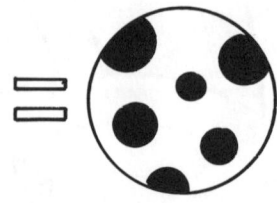

What have you written?

Did you know...?
Italy is famous for pasta, as well as pizzas!
Some kinds of pasta are named after their shapes:

ravioli = cushions   *spaghetti = little strings*

vermicelli = little worms

The Big Boot of Italy
Kicked little Sicily

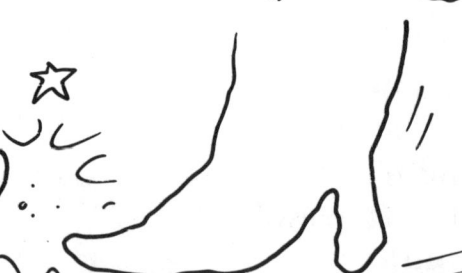

Into the middle
Of the Mediterranean   Sea!

Can you see why someone made up this rhyme about Italy?

32